Until There Is Nothing Left

UNTIL THERE IS NOTHING LEFT

Gary Metras

⌘

The Writer's Voice
RIDGEWAY PRESS
Roseville, Michigan
2003

First Edition

ISBN 1-56439-119-1

Acknowledgments:

The Acre: Shampoo, After the 2000 Vote, Looking for the Men's Room at the All Girl's College, *Beyond Doggerel:* Child in Winter, Bull Thistle Press Folder Editions: A Lazy Summer Night, *Circus Maximus:* Exercise Walk at the Veterans Hospital, *Common Ground Review:* The State Hospital, *Connecticut Poetry Review:* The Last Lighthouse, *5AM:* Essay on Weather, *The Greenfield Review:* The History of Mirrors, *Jack the Daw:* Coffee, Lost Histories, *Larcom Review:* Watching My Father Sleep in His 74th Year, *Lungfish Review:* It's Like a Fancy Shirt, Scenes: Some with Motion, The Coming of It, *Perimeter:* The Spell, *Potlatcxh:* Counterpoise, *Place of the Long River: A Connecticut River Anthology* (Glastonbury, CT: Blue Moon Press): View of the Connecticut River Valley from the Summit House, Mt. Holyoke, *Pulpsmith:* Mishaps on Delancey Street, *Sahara:* Dementia in December, *The Signal:* Dunes.

The author also thanks M. L. Liebler of Ridgeway Press for support of this project.

The Writer's Voice
The YMCA of Metropolitan Detroit
(a member of the National Writer's Voice Project
of the YMCA of USA)
and
RIDGEWAY PRESS
P.O. Box 120
Roseville, MI 48066

For Natalie

Contents

The Last Lighthouse

They say men once lived in them
behind white clapboard
beneath the white tower,
that nothing could stop
their belief in light,
not the worst Nor'easter on record,
not fog so still and solid
only angels could move,
and not the boredom
that drives men mad.
They say some brought wives
to soften those rocks,
that children were born there
who battened tears in storms,
who learned the rhythm of breath
from the rhythm of waves,
and who came to believe
wind carried them everywhere
they could not go.

Cave

Even here: tiny hearts in the thick dark,
pale roots beneath damp rock.
Even here: hollow rhythms of water,
a drip at a time, a clock that nibbles stone
or constructs stone. Even here:
light carried through rocky cracks
on the backs of spiders,
or leaked in mineral dribbles
through weak veins.
Even here the struggle: multiplied:
blind fish in the heavy stream,
eyeless worms in stony soil,
hanging fur in the tight air
of blind fate.

Lost Histories

There are writings on stone
no one knows:

scratched accounts of births or deaths,
of acres or animals bought or lost,
stick figures upright in wealth or war,
and songs so immortal

only stones
should sing them,

as we cannot, bewildered in our museums,
lost in the ruins of our left brain
where unresolved questions
stain like acidic rain

on stone
only fingers can read.

The State Hospital

The neighborhood people walking home
from shopping downtown never look
at those windows with their bars.
They teach their children parading home
from school to look straight ahead
or at their shoes until they pass
that brick monstrosity with those bars
on the windows, and from where,
every now and then, someone
would scream as if an arm was being
ripped off, or a brain sucked out
through the nose. And hearing that scream
the children would run the rest of the way
home, certain that the fears leaking
inside their skulls, that the threats
of their parents to eat all the peas at supper
and say their prayers at bedtime
were as real as bars on windows.

After the 2000 Vote

Someone is speaking on TV
but it isn't enough to stop
the mind from digging into
the mulch that is the forest
floor where a centipede
crawls through lumps of decay
in search of happiness.
If only it could tell us
what makes it happy,
we wouldn't have to get dirty.
If only the speaker loved truth
more than himself,
or loved words as much
as himself, or at least
said "shit" on camera
once or twice, maybe
then I'd listen.

The History of Mirrors

When first things are
indeed first, consider the sun,
impassive source of mirrors,
self exposure its one
delight, as it hangs there,
holding worlds to itself
and displaying all it has,
generous as a creator bored
with creation.

The sky, a blue
prismatic substance, a prophet,
doing what it must to light,
even when half the cosmic
is illusion, and the other
clear only in darkness,
wanted to keep it all.

Clouds moved in to shade
the visions and ended up
watering down light to drop it,
like fragments of a lens, a relic,
to the rocky crust just
becoming self sure.

There were gaps in what thoughts
the stone had, where floods
congregated, their rumor
of privilege spawning

as they reflected the elliptic
in litanies of its only
repeating message, a chorus
all inherited.

And when that boy leaned
over the grassy bank
of the exhausted pool
to get a look, everything changed.

Exercise Walk at the Veterans Hospital

They go in file, with studied suspicion,
eying the ground as if still bewildered
in minefields in Normandy. Their heads
low-hung, the faces and bodies full
of useless bones draped with skin pale
as the white coat of the attendant leading
their way from one solemn building to
another. They shy away from him, cringe
at his touch, knowing the battlefield
butcher steps among the dead and wounded,
his hands gleaming with saws. One vet
stops out of line, out of order; his
pants sag at the waist but barely reach
his socks; suspenders haul the dead
weight; it is their duty; a small favor.
He lights a cigarette that isn't there
and stares at pools of water at curbside
to see himself duck into foxholes
at Iwo Jima. A buddy taps his shoulder;
he obeys some inner command and falls,
letting the camouflage drop from eyes
that refuse any more, submitting to winds
like an island in hurricane. The squad
crowds around. Still they sympathize
with battle-weary minds that slip away
from the shelling and enter a world
they all know. They gather him up.
March on. And talk without tone about
two on a match.

Mishaps on Delancey Street

1
Flames snake out the block's blown windows.
Something old is born again in fury.
Eyes on the street ignite. A loose crowd
knots. Each one passes awe and fear
to the next person until none are
strangers. Linked by this sharing spectacle,
this need to witness without names,
their eyes stare, widen, become a single
flame as the whole neighborhood blazes.

2
The cry of brakes and tires on the dark,
dark pavement sticks in the ribs and
breathing is impossible until the luring sound
thuds into someone else. People gather.
Shoulders press to instant familiarity, to
body odors made public. Bits of headlight glass
quash under someone's shoe. Blood will stain
another before it leaves a faint trail into
    concrete
distances and this destiny we share.

Essay on Weather

The weather doesn't matter
to someone bent on greatness.
The rough seas did not stop D-Day,
nor the bombs that fell on Berlin,
nor the pills, or the bullet, or the immolation
Hitler swallowed. Three times dead
and he was spotted twelve years later
getting into a cab one rainy day
in Buenos Aires. The weather was immaterial
though gusting to thirty-five mph
that June 27th as Bryan Berg set the last
card atop the hundred and five storey house of
cards,
in the school's gym; that's seven hundred
decks of playing cards; that's thirty-six thousand
four hundred cards held one at a time
like a child's hand; the big bad wolf
would not huff and puff down your house
because he's been banished from reality,
or is it superseded by greater cruelties.
Oh, to be the Boston Red Sox in October
as they suck in the autumn breeze
and hit run after run after run
into the record book and still lose.
Oh, to be Apryl Scott in Michigan in November
as her fingers knotted with the last stitch
that put her rag doll, an inch shy of forty-two feet,
into the record book; yes, it's just a doll,
but for years her needle disappeared

into cloth like some abstraction,
perhaps mending the world's pain;
at least the present mind assumes such,
being basically optimistic. But what to make
of thirty-one years chewing gum,
of folding and bending those colored wrappers
and silver liners into a chain eighteen thousand
seven hundred and twenty one feet long?
Yes, Gary Duschl, enraptured since 1965 by this
need,
driven by this need whether you named it or not,
despite the blizzards and floods and calm, cloudless
days,
you now are known outside your little hometown
of Waterdown, Ontario, for what it's worth,
thanks to the Guiness Records people
and their tireless efforts to catalog our greatness,
to hold up to the face of war and famine,
tornado and hurricane, bombings and shootings,
these little acts, idle as they are, idiosyncratic, selfish
even,
acted out beneath that great wheel of sun and moon
turning its weather over our labors.

Outside the Dakota

(with John Pompei)

A March breeze stings
the ears like the cry
of John Lennon's soul
as his body collapsed
on the sidewalk and
his soul joined the air,
lifted above the carnage,
looked back, briefly,
as color drained
from spilled blood,
as a woman screamed,
and a pistol fell
to pavement, lifted until
everything he ever said,
did, and thought became
the air we breathe.

It's Like a Fancy Shirt

From the clear air of October
I enter the kitchen
to the smell of food
cooked hours ago

and remember how carefully
you once folded cloth diapers
fresh from the wash.
It's like my fancy shirt

that, years later,
became a cleaning rag, and how,
washing windows,
you leaned into the wet glass

and your shirt grew thinner
and your nipples harder.
I smiled and smile again.

The Argument as Tahitian Metaphor

Like bamboo, I bend
in the wind of your words,
my hollow core becomes
a chamber to echo storms
as the barometric pressure
of emotions rise.

I could fall, like a palm tree,
from the typhoon in your voice,
my shallow roots will rest
atop the earth at your feet
and begin, so soon, to wither
in the heat of your tropics.

So, my love, we argue again.
Sometime I swear you do this
just to fulfill our pledge
those many years ago
to make love after every fight.
Yes, put on your grass shirt.

The Mischief of Blueberries

"The hour's amenities are all to me"
—Edna St. Vincent Millay

If a ghost thrills our winter nights amid
sheetrock and clapboard, cabinets and curtains,
and if its moan echoes across the church nave
without effect, there is justice in the made world.
If one speaks of love at midnight, and the words
spark in the soul the way the noon sun beckons
apple blossoms in May, then there is meaning
to brain and bone and heart. And always
eloquence is my lips on yours, like the breeze
that sings in the maple tree in June, as graduates
let fall from pale shoulders their dark robes. And if
we endure the mischief of blueberries staining
our fingers to enjoy that sweetness on
the tongue, there is purpose for this leafy world.

How Perfect

The man sitting in the next booth
is telling his half empty coffee cup,
"...isolation is my true identity."
I don't mean to eavesdrop, but I am.
I don't mean to have no trust in the universe,
but don't.
I signal the waitress.
I want to tell her my cup is empty,
but I blurt out,
"I stole all the iambic pentameters from the
Library of Congress."
The man in the next booth pays no attention.
The waitress simply says,
"That was decaf, right."
I nod, afraid to open my mouth again.
When she returns with the steaming pot,
she leans perfume-close and whispers,
"All that happens is an expression of my
perfection."
She walks back behind the counter.
My eyes follow her, noticing for the first time
how perfect her walk is.
The man in the next booth says,
"It's all illusion."

After the Dance

In the photograph the gypsy girl
holds in her right hand a tambourine
straight above her head like a halo.
She holds it for what comes next.
The left arm angles out to the side,
left toe points and holds the pose
before she twirls her body:
It is then the waist long hair
will flow like a widening smile
and her skirts will billow
and a man sitting at one
of the small wooden tables
drinking his cognac and cola
will fall in love, will approach her
after the dance with words
too beautiful to retell.
She will leave with him,
will walk into the dark night
clutching his arm.
Her father will stand in silence
a few moments in his empty café
as colorless as an old photograph
before he gently lifts
from the floor the dropped halo.

A Lazy Summer Night

The wind sings in the wine bottle.

We lounge on the grass in the back yard
to watch the full moon lift above
our small horizon.

We sip and hold hands
even after all these years of marriage.

The talk is simple. The stars tardy.

A lone firefly blinks its own
small moon against the black of the trees.

As the moon rises light spills on us
and wind sings a familiar tune
we hum together.

"What Do You Love?"

I'm sitting on the beach
with two beautiful women
born in Europe. One asks me,
"Was liebt dich?"

I turn from her
and face the horizon
where air and water touch.
My body presses into sand.

How elemental,
I think and wonder
where the fire is, that friction
that will burst into flame

and consume us?
I lie back down.
My leg brushes Natalka's thigh.
A gull, overhead, suddenly

turns and dives
for a silver flash in the wave.
I say to Ulrike, "The moment.
It is the moment I love."

The Night We Didn't Make Love

I skim my hand over my sleeping wife's breast.
The nipple hardens.

I slide my hand along her ribs onto her hip.
She has a flu—I shouldn't wake her.

Her body warms the darkness,
soothes the desire.

I rest my face so it touches the back of her hair
and sleep.

Across the Blackened Vine

"I tell you this across the blackened vine."
—Edna St. Vincent Millay

The close sky entombs us—we walk
between limits and we think without wind
that no ghost will pass through the wall
of our torn kiss to hound us in its very cry,
in its breast like a groomed beast, or some
Beauty fleeing across the meadow of the mind
toward the cliffs with their hollow wall of air,
with that joyous fear of gravity in the plunge
toward self, toward all that is holy
and loving, all that porous emotion
cascading around us, around each foot fall
that splinters the dew as we try to run
past the moment, past the rain blossoming
in the mirror, in the cavity of the heart.

Dementia in December

Winter trees a circle
of bare pain
splinters of ice
barbed
wire of heaven
Bird
Bird
Bird
everywhere
lose their song
in the bushes
Their eye
stares
everywhere

A feather falls black
a feather falls blue

Spit in the hand
freezes
Snowflake
in the hand
melts
A silver nail
an icicle
in the staunch air
The heart an easy target

brick
brick
brick
brick

That old tower hides
        a rusty maiden

  Lurk
          in the bushes
  Lurk
          in the bushes
  Lurk
          in the bushes
                              songless

Christmas Moon

It is the moon,
    full and solsticing,
as it hangs between dirty clouds
    that marks the season,

that spreads its round joy
through the dark waves
    of a boy's guilt and doubt,

that shines alike on reindeer,
tree, and the child,
    who carefully set
the plate of three cookies
    on the corner of the table,

because
    the coming storm
cannot eclipse the desire.

Child in Winter

Today I dress you in white
because it snowed last night.

White outside. White inside.

You drift through the house
like blowing snow.

When I catch you, you become
a snowgirl,

arms, legs, whole body
gone stiff.

I touch my lips
to your pale cheek.

You melt.

White outside.
And inside

two pools of laughter.

Her Hair

The way the light
reflects
on her barrette—
jewels
in the eye of a beholder
The way the bangs
curl in studied
chaos across the forehead—
a smile
that knows
more than it says
So unlike her sister—
straight and tinted and tucked behind
the ears—
as sensible
as the solar system
—a place for every
planet
every passion

The Spell

It was Louisiana rain falling
on Massachusetts snow in January
and warm and cold wrestled
and fog lifted from the snow pack on the hayfield,
rose up in small, white puffs
like the souls of all who died in winter,
rose like the spell said they would
and the south breeze steered them further north,
further to the frozen zones
beyond the reach of any wind,
of any rain or warmth,
beyond anything except the words
of an old woman
in a darkened room a block
behind Bourbon Street
rattling her necklace of bones.

Shampoo

"I say your
hair can be
outrageous,"
is the promise of
the advertisement
in the magazine.
Does it mean
they know the formula
for happiness?
Have they
discovered the hidden
protein
of the soul?
The model is
spread across
the bottom of the page
with a look
that says: I know
the secret of
hair,
armpits,
lips,
money.

Coffee

There is never enough coffee
or poetry to last the night.
The smell as flat as bad
language.
One sip and sad similes
stick in the throat.
So stale and automatic,
brewed in easy machines.
We suffer two lumps of
metaphor
and non-dairy cream
as bland as TV imagery.
But this is America.
We are comfortable.
We have sacrificed everything
for comfort. Some say
the Russians still know
how to brew it and their
mouths
are full of it.
When our mouths stink,
we wash them clean
as the whistle
of a tea pot.

New Year's Eve

It's a clear night sky
    becoming overcast.
            One year cycles
into another.
    Glasses clink together
            at the Oyster Bar
and if a few drops spill,
    all the better—
            a blessing
                    to vanishing stars.
The sound of explosions
    in the air above the Commons.
            The smell
                    of sulfur in the air.
Lights go out
    on Newbury Street
as the flash of fireworks bounce
    off clouds.

    In the morning
            confetti
                    strewn everywhere
along Commonwealth Avenue
    like a panic of joy,
            or a long sigh

because everything
    is still the way it was
            only older.

12-31-99

January 10th

The sky mad at the world.
Wind and rain and snow.
Fog and freeze. The toaster
refuses to make the bagel
brown and crusty. A large
coffee to go. All the cars
slowing. All the birds stuck
to trees, their blue breath
icicling the air. The radio
just banter. The wiper blades
streaking the windshield
faster than the defroster.
All the cars ahead braking
all the way downhill.
The backs of necks tensing
as if the boss was looking
over your shoulder. Thirty
minutes to drive eight miles.
Under tomorrow's sun
this will be another
world, glistening, like
diamonds under glass.

Looking for the Men's Room at the All Girl's College

The woman poet talks a long time
about Paris, El Salvador, and motherhood

before she reads the first poem where she teases
her hair as a 60s teen in Michigan.

The distance between things more vast
than her extended arm, than her 90s hair,

flat and fallen to shoulders slightly rounded
by the weight of lines on paper,

by the heavy air of words, by the pause stretched
in inhale, by experience trapped in memory.

Afterward, I walk corridors and stairwells
for what seems hours, too embarrassed

to stop one of the girls, who are everywhere,
for directions. The few men in the crowd

are as distressed as I, leaning against walls,
or pointing with their faces to the exit.

When I meet the poet, herself, at the reception,
I say nothing of this, then hurry out.

Manhood

The day after the boy
got his driver's license,
he said to his father,
"Dad, I'm sixteen. I've got
my license. I'm a man.
I don't have to listen to you."
The father replied, "Son,
that's not the way it works.
It goes like this: You get
one punch; if you knock me down,
you don't have to do what I say.
But if I don't go down,
I get one punch."
The boy didn't think about it;
he made a fist and swung.
His father's head rocked back
and his body swayed
but he didn't go down.
Then the father said, "My turn."

Classic Car

A man drives his '62 Vette downtown.
The top down, August 2nd, a perfect day.

The exhaust rumbles.
The car shines like candy in a jar.

Everyone on the street and in their cars turn and look.
He revs the engine as he passes the old factory

and a flock of pigeons rises from the ground,
circles the dirty brick smokestack and settles

on the roof to watch the car glide toward Main Street.
The man smiles as if he had opened a jar of candy.

Dunes

There is something magic about the desert.
Not the sight of unending dunes.
Dunes are a refrain in the downpour of sun,
a whisper repeating—The next dune
is the last.

You enter the desert an ark
hauling all there is.
Direction is suspect
and too soon hopes deepen for green
over the next dune.

The sun burns the center of sky to a white gold.
A vision forms in this silence,
in that distance
only a step away, hidden
by the next dune.

Stumbling along, sand shifts underfoot
like another choice. The sun
becomes an unavoidable halo
and the tongue sleeps, swollen,
unable to say—
Eden.
High up
something breaks heaven; a dark spot
descends, circling close.
And wind confesses incredibly white bones
in the lull of the next dune.

The impotence, like a martyr without

attendants,
is worst. Humanity
out there
is the line,
vertical
against odds, as it
falters, as the rhythm lenticulates,
and the voice commands—
the next dune. The next dune.

And what grail dreams in the desert sands?
And what woman of healing charms
abides the arid times
to quench this spirit of man
as she waits beyond that last
dune?

View of the Connecticut River Valley from the Summit House, Mt. Holyoke

From here everything is order and purpose.
The sky that loafs atop surrounding hills
makes the valley seem more flat than it is.

The river that cut the valley floor
keeps Hadley from becoming Northampton
and they like it that way.

Though the traffic between the towns
across the Coolidge Bridge is heavy,
cars stop and go without sound,

with red brake lights shining ornament
and not arrested destination. Down there,
the brown and yellow farm fields

of the Meadows, newly emptied of corn
and potato, make sense in size and range,
tapering as each steers toward the river

and the memory of flood. Right below,
Mitch's Island grows longer with silt
and on its leeward side, where salmon once

relaxed from the current, the water
is more shallow and more empty.
Over there the interstate highway bisects

the oxbow. Do the men wearing ties who carry
calculators and protractors between offices
still think we must divide and conquer?

And there, the university, with its towers
a cluster of brick, steel and concrete mountains,
does it train such men right now?

This is the first time I've walked
all the way up on the paved road
that winds around the mountain where

South Hadley, Holyoke, Chicopee and Springfield
are visible in more than biography.
When I stopped, half-way, for rest and relief,

there were dusty blueberries dangling
from browning stems that stuck out
of a rock ledge at chest height.

Touched by November frost, they were bitter.
I set my face as one with ambition, pumped the
arms,
and paced the last leg up. I met none

but a scraggly black and white cat
who cried once with the look of all
the hungry babies in those cities below.

Down there the line of red brick factories
of Easthampton points to the river
where its waste once flowed.

Some worker probably leans on the iron rail
of the loading dock as his cigarette's ash
grows longer while he stares at the tenements

across the street where his wife has tea
and talks to the neighbor about money or sex.
Idleness accomplished, he returns to work.

I am resting against the white wood balustrade
on the veranda of this old resort. Long
minutes pass in surveillance. The sun falls

behind Turkey Hill in Westhampton.
As the air whispers about winter, I say,
all my life lives here.

The Coming of It

I flick the spider away
with my shoe. It lands
three feet from where I sit

writing a letter. It rests there
a half minute and crawls off,
one leg bent wrong. Then a dying

moth hops and flits on the floor
toward me. When I brush it
with the same shoe,

its meager body collapses into dust
and bits of angled wing.
Neither saw it coming.

How could they know, any more than
the man driving on the bridge
about to fall.

Scenes: Some with Motion

i.
Zen monks at Kenrokuen
sweep algae
off river rocks
to clean the water for golden carp,
the wealth
of the soul.

Watching them
knee-deep in water,
straw brooms in hand,
a child
laughs.

ii.
In Minnesota snow
falls to the slope
of a horse's ear.
It's enough to make
a grown man leave
his body.

iii.
Rain pools on granite steps
in New York City
and reflects
a stone church
as the spire talks to
God in the clouds.

A woman, leaving
the confessional, steps
in the puddle.

There are rings of water
growing from her heel,
then just the rings,
then the water,
then reflection.

iv.

An empty cup
is left in a sink
in Massachusetts.
The faucet leaks.
Once the cup fills,
it is spilled.

It will fill again.

And be empty again.

Nocturnal

Beneath the moon in Africa, a dry river
dreams and the giraffe grows small.

Beneath the moon in Africa, a man
sits by a smoking pot of alligator stew,

knowing the beauty of juice-black teeth
and how pale bones become.

Beneath the moon in Africa, shadows
moan for the broken tusks,

winds pause in the beaks of flamingos
asleep on one thin leg,

and a cheetah cries to hear her own voice
beneath the moon in Africa.

Learning To Lie at the Zoo

The tiger naps in his cage.
Tall, yellow grasses sway in his dream.
He waits for wind
to bring the smell of buffalo.

When he stirs and looks about he'll not
at first remember where he is.
The horizon falls across his eyes
in striped shadows of bars. He smells
the easy horse meat tossed by human hands
and slowly walks toward it.

Somewhere in the lost
continent of those eyes
a roar bursts, muscles
tense to leap in
open air and
claws tear flesh.

The children only see its size—
paws large as their faces,
fangs like forearms,
a hunger only hinted at.
Better now to move to the next cage.

Staring at Nothing

I'm standing in the middle of the road tonight,
listening to the gentle noise dried leaves make
tumbling down the asphalt in the slight
October breeze. An overcast sky prevents
the moonlight from doing its job. There is
a mist falling or rising. It's hard to tell.
I see dark movement out of the corner of an eye.
A shadow crosses the road behind me.

I feel that if I move or turn toward it,
I will regret what happens. It is difficult
to stare at nothing. Then the sound of branches
at roadside bending and springing back.
Then leaves skirting down the street.
Then footsteps toward my dark house.

Watching My Father Sleep in His 74th Year

For the longest time I stood by the bed
thinking I did this at age eight
as he coughed and thrashed
and I was frightened and we both prayed
to the demons of the dark for relief or release,
but this day as I watched I thought he was not real,
an immobile impostor of a loud and woolly man,
—not even the eyes could force the closed lids
to shudder—as dreamless as a tree,
or the chimneys he'd built, unlike
anything he is now, lying here on his back,
with breath so shallow you could walk
through the pool of his emphysema'd air
and not get wet, or not skip stones across
the surface of his sunken chest without breaking
something, like the day my young brother
batted a stone through the neighbor's kitchen
    window
and my old man made me confess, being eldest son,
and I did confess and prayed to the train passing
in the background, its whistle knifing the air,
its vanishing a lump in the throat. In six months
I would stand here again for the longest time
before I took his cold, cold hand in mine,
before the others entered the room.

Easter 2001

> "having sown the iron seeds of Autogeddon"
> —Lawrence Ferlinghetti

I'm driving into the face of Autogeddon
with acid rain dancing on the windshield
            It's a dance of exhaustion
It's a Freeway
but someone will pay
            When the clouds sail east
Smog hugging the noon sun
Smog painting the sunset
            in hues of otherness that are us
Red sky of morning
Sailor take warning
            The good ship Earth
sailing through the vacuum of space
with its one almost holy race
                        America's Cup
runneth over into a petrochemical
nightmare
            The sleepwalker always smiles
as he steps to the edge

            and beyond

Flying to Detroit

for M. L. Liebler

At fifteen thousand feet Lake Ontario still
    looks Great, but Niagara Falls
was a white line rippling the jade river.
    And Buffalo?—just shades of rust.

It is here the land flattens, and all
    the ground-blinded designs begin:
Squares and rectangles,
    green and tan and brown blocks
progressing across the April chilled
    vision to the Lake's edge.

Highways and roads arc and bisect
    their way through
the geometry of our lives,
    houses and fields and malls
of this land as level as water—
    one more flat plane of existence
the mind digests until it becomes
    as natural as breathing.

I think of all the high school
    students on the ground, slouching
in square-topped desks
    lined or circled within a square room,
itself within a larger square
    and so on

until multiplication becomes
    as natural as breathing,

and so on until all the students
    hate Shakespeare,
hate math, hate parents and police,
    hate asparagus, the Beach Boys,
hate Volkswagon Beetles, and so on,
    even unto the hair, lips
and nose staring back at them
    from mirrors

because they know what life
    is like, that attractive people
win. And the rest?— losers
    or merely players
in someone else's game, on someone
    else's team,

but the bullet or the shrapnel
    tears any skin,
because every generation of Americans
    tastes war, and war
swallows
    them.

I could become cynical
    thinking all this,
then remember it is Saturday
    over Ohio,

no school,
    and the older teens have already
worked hours at doughnut shops
    learning the physics

of coffee and dollars and time,
    while others dress
for the lunch rush
    in corporate kitchens
and franchised counters
    where minutes and months
have warped into nothing
    Einstein could formulate,

and younger kids switch
    cartoons to pixels pretending
to goblins, orcs and dragons,
    who are neither friend
nor teacher, mother nor coach
    in a world reduced
to couch and digits clicking faster,
    more agile, into a blur
of someone named Newton
    who started it all.

The blue firmament of Milton
    whitens.
Meteorology becomes law, becomes
    the discourse of the day
where smartly dressed blondes
    and slick-haired men
compete with God
    to know how things will be—

clouds do their job,
    envelope airplanes, render sightless

passengers and crew
    so that truth becomes electronics
waving us down
    through fourteen thousand feet
of blind faith
    and barometric pressure falling.

The jarring drop and lock
    of landing gear breaks
each pilgrim's prayer,
    and tidy suburbs revealed
unto us,
    with their rows of new houses
packed end on end
    within a neat square as if this
the only way to live,
    and executive half acre lawns
come into view,
    but again just squares within a square,
only larger,

    then highway and bare trees,
swamp and runway,
    and light rain
everywhere,
    except
        M. L.'s smile.

Counterpoise

Every perception does not need a conception.
Some mornings it's easier to swim in cloud
than the Connecticut River.

The mountain here is so old
its volcanic crater is lost to time.
Once I freed a trilobite from its flank.

The mountain is 1,202 feet above sea level.
In the year 1212 the Children's Crusade began.
A thousand children entered a dream
and never woke up.

Some things don't even know their own deaths.
Billions of arthropods are only stones.
The mountain is held in place by clouds
and the weight of carp in the river.

The Vine

"...she wanted to paint the Bay of Naples some day..."
—O Henry, "The Last Leaf"

In the dull world
we dream a sun sets beyond water in
a foreign country,

a sun sinking with our breath that diminishes
in the mechanics of daily life.
Earth turns and tilts

and at the first frosty wind leaves fall in bunches,
then one by one.
We pray for the loving

deceits of friends to keep
the last leaf
whole and green, clinging to the vine

against all privation
until we rise from the sick bed,
lift our body from the sick bed

to get the tools we need,
a bowl of soup, paper and pen, brush and palette,
and fix the illusion, the life we crave.

Tenth Birthday

On the birthday boy's dresser, a Flying Fortress
in progress with soon-to-be working ball turret,
retractable landing gear, ground crew with bombs
to paint and load imaginations. Just a childhood

unwinding under the Cold War. Just a plastic
model to join the others hanging on fishing line
from the ceiling: Thunderbolt, Lightning,
Spitfire roaring across the blue sky of dreams.

And on the wall a poster of silhouettes
of soviet airplanes he's memorized to win
a merit badge and warn the country against
first attack. Just another birthday, with Sputnik

a few months away. Then Mercury Capsule.
The Berlin Airlift. The Bay of Pigs. And Tet,
and all that. Young Republicans in his high school
will wear Barry Goldwater for President buttons.

But not for years. Today the boy lies on the grass
below the air base as silver Stratofortress,
one after another, take off in clouds of noise
and carbon exhaust that fall to where he lay

before he, too, left the ground.

The Geese of Swan River

for Jan and Denny Gurn

Geese glide on Swan River at Dennisport,
paddling against the incoming tide
and a gray dusk in angled file as if still in flight.
No one remembers when swans last
swam this river, but geese are here,
searching for what makes them happy.
The ice cream eaten, I shred the cone
to a hundred pieces, throw them
from the bridge and the coherent line
dissembles as geese scramble to feed,
then alewives break the water's surface
for what is left. At midnight we sit on the beach
as the full moon's light dilutes the ocean
the way a painter's brush, tinted white
at last, transforms the dark, dark sea.
High above us, geese honk
their joy or fear. Then darkness, itself,
pulling the light. Then clouds constricting
the moon until there is nothing left
but a faint glow like a broken halo far out
on the night's water, then that, too, is gone,
and the only light are pale faces
on the beach growing older together.

About the Author

Gary Metras has taught high school English for thirty-one years. He has also worked as store clerk, short order cook, mason's tender, Air Traffic Controller (U. S. Air Force 1966 - 1970), and book store manager. He holds degrees from the University of Massachusetts at Amherst and Goddard College. He books of poems are *The Night Watches* (1981) and *Destiny's Calendar* (1985) and ten chapbooks, most recently *Today's Lesson* (1997). His poems, essays and reviews have appeared in such periodicals as *The American Voice, Another Chicago Magazine, The Bellingham Review, Boston Review of Books, Connecticut Poetry Review, English Journal, Larcom Review, Negative Capability, North Dakota Quarterly, Poetry, Poetry East, Small Press Review* and *Yankee*. He is a fine press printer and the editor and publisher of Adastra Press. He lives in Easthampton, Massachusetts.